# AMERICAN BOY

# AMERICAN BOY

## The Story of
# TIM SCHUT

THRONE
PUBLISHING GROUP

Throne Publishing
1601 E 69th St #306,
Sioux Falls, SD 57108

# TABLE OF CONTENTS

*Introduction* . . . . . . . . . . . . . . . . . . . . . . . . . . . . . *vii*

1. All American Boy . . . . . . . . . . . . . . . . . . . . . . 1

2. Coming of Age . . . . . . . . . . . . . . . . . . . . 13

3. My Bride – Jen . . . . . . . . . . . . . . . . . . . . . 19

4. Growing A Family . . . . . . . . . . . . . . . . . . . . 23

   Pictures . . . . . . . . . . . . . . . . . . . . . . . . . . . 29

5. Success Principles . . . . . . . . . . . . . . . . . . . 57

6. Business and Career . . . . . . . . . . . . . . . . . . 65

7. Community Involvement . . . . . . . . . . . . . . . . 71

8. Mentors . . . . . . . . . . . . . . . . . . . . . . . . . . 79

9. A Message to My Family . . . . . . . . . . . . . . . . 93

*Afterword* . . . . . . . . . . . . . . . . . . . . . . . . . . . *105*

# INTRODUCTION

In June 2020, I noticed my superpower, speech, becoming just a touch more difficult for me. The words weren't coming out correctly. And that wasn't me. I asked my dentist friend what could be causing my troubles. Something dental, perhaps? He suggested I visit a doctor and get checked, which I did in August, 2020. The doctor prescribed speech therapy and a brain MRI, which was clear. I continued faithfully with speech therapy and attributed my struggles to stress at work.

The first doctor I saw referred me to neurology at Sanford, and they tested me for everything—multiple sclerosis, lyme disease, and more. In the meantime, I quit my job because I thought the stress of managing a team was getting the best of me. Yet even after leaving my job, my speech didn't improve.

By May 2021, the Sanford neurologist referred me to Mayo Clinic. My original appointment was scheduled for August 17, but I called every morning at 8 a.m. to see if there were any cancellations. On June 21, 2021, I got into the Mayo Clinic in Rochester, Minnesota, for testing. The ALS doctor ran me through several tests. He said, "I don't think you have ALS, but we're going to continue to do the ALS testing." He then added, "I'd like you to meet with one of our speech pathologists." Within forty minutes she had me diagnosed: primary progressive apraxia of speech. It's a rare condition affecting less than one in a million people. When the speech pathologist spoke those words, we had no clue what the diagnosis meant. My wife, Jen, kept taking notes, and I just listened as they spoke.

Jen and I left the doctor's office, ate an early lunch, read up on the disease, and cried together. The next few days were a blur, as I gave approximately thirty vials of blood for test after test. They also performed a spinal tap. We stayed in Rochester for a week, and the tests confirmed the speech pathologist's initial diagnosis. I decided to volunteer for a study at Mayo on this disease. Only twenty-eight people are currently in it, and I am the youngest person without an underlying condition. This study has been going on for twelve years, and less than one hundred participants are involved. Aside from the diagnosis, the doctor simply said, "Eat right, exercise, remain social, and talk a lot."

From that moment forward, our lives changed forever.

While at the Mayo, Jen said, "I think we should move back home."

I immediately knew she was right. We'd owned a farmhouse near Wentworth, South Dakota, for about seven years, and we dreamed of retiring there. Our life in Sioux Falls was fast and furious, and we needed to simplify and slow down. So we did. We sold our house in Sioux Falls, packed up everything, and moved to the farmhouse. Our girls started school in Chester, and our family adjusted to our new normal. Jen loves being closer to her parents, and I love seeing our girls thrive in a rural school system. Moving to the farm was the right decision. Our life has slowed down, and we're focusing on our family. We have more intimacy and don't miss our old life's hustle and bustle.

You see, my diagnosis didn't just come with answers. It also came with an adjusted life expectancy. My condition is a degenerative brain disorder, and if what the doctors say is true, I could be gone in ten to fifteen years. Shocking right? Oddly enough, I wasn't shocked to hear this news. I've always had a feeling I was destined for a shorter-than-average life expectancy.

"Why?" you might ask.

When I was eight- or nine-years-old, I was playing in the trees behind our house, next to the church, and I heard a voice say, "Tim, you're going to die young." It startled and scared me at the time, but I took it seriously. I suspect it was God giving me a glimpse of the plan for my life. I took it to heart, and I've aimed to live every day to the fullest. I thought of that moment in the trees when I heard this diagnosis.

I don't know how many years I have left on this earth, but what I do know is that I have a rare and unique opportunity. From this moment until I take my last breath, I have the opportunity to love my family, serve my community, and help everyone I can help—and what a privilege to have that time!

# CHAPTER ONE

# ALL AMERICAN BOY

Hello World!

I was born at 8 a.m. on October 4, 1976, in Dell Rapids, South Dakota. My mom, Pam, was eighteen-years-old and my dad, Dale, was twenty. The doctor told my parents, "It's a boy!" then the nurses proceeded to put a bracelet on my wrist reading "Baby Girl Schut." It's a funny memory now because, trust me, I was very much a boy!

I was raised in a rural area of Eastern South Dakota. The first place I remember living is the Severson place. Bud Severson lived in a trailer with his wife, Lorraine. Bud, whose real name was Lorraine, just like his wife, had a woodshop, and my brother, Pat, and I would go in there and "help" him out—if you can call two little kids "helpers." Bud made us a desk, and we had that thing forever. I wonder if it's still around.

After that, we moved to the house that my grandparents owned, next to St. Jacobs Church. I still remember my fifth birthday at the house; my birthday cake had a wind-up alligator on top of it. I remember winding it up and having it "eat" my cake. My fifth birthday was a milestone one for me. I wore ugly, brown corrective shoes until age five, and I'll never forget getting my first pair of regular shoes. They were gray, and we bought them at the JC Penney store in Madison.

Not far from our home stood a dive bar and restaurant called "Buffalo Trading Post," and I remember my friends and me riding our dirt bikes down to the store and renting movies. The owner had the option to start a "tab" at the restaurant, and he kept one open for me. Of course, I didn't have a clue about money or paying bills, so one day the owner called my dad and said, "Are you going to pay your tab?"

My dad said, "What tab?"

Turns out Pat, and I had run up a pretty stout bill for cheese balls and chicken strips, and they tasted awesome.

Around age ten, my friends and I started a bicycle "gang" where we rode our bikes to each others' houses or to the Buffalo Trading Post. The members were Kathy, Jeff, Pat, and myself. Kathy's mom, Ila, made us t-shirts using tubes of fabric paint that said, *Hot Wheels burning rubber*. We kept the gang going for about three years.

My family moved three times while I was young, and eventually settled about a half-mile south of my paternal grandparents' farm. Oddly enough, the house we moved into became available for rent, because the man who lived there before us murdered his wife. Yikes!

My mom was the part-time, paid secretary for Colton Lutheran Parish, which is made up of First Lutheran in Colton and St. Jacobs in rural Colton. As a family, we stuffed many newsletters and folded bulletins. We even mowed the church lawn. One of my early memories is singing at Bethel Lutheran Home in Madison and going to Pizza Hut afterwards. We loved doing that, especially with our favorite pastor, Roy Rierson, and his wife, Estelle. Roy was a big Chicago Cubs fan. Out of all the congregations Roy served, he chose to be buried in St. Jacobs Cemetery, and as a congregation we felt honored.

My mom also worked at Dakota State College, now DSU, in Madison, South Dakota, where she was always giving and helpful to other people. As well, she volunteered us to move professors in or out. We spent many weekends helping unload or load moving trucks. I don't remember her having hobbies, because she was so busy chasing us kids around. She was focused on her family and serving others.

My dad could be found either farming or working at Gehl Manufacturing. Both of my parents had full-time "city jobs" and farmed full-time on the side. Saturdays were my days to spend time with Dad at the farm. I loved riding on the tractor with him. Without fail, Grandma Schut had a brown paper bag filled with candy and a pack of baseball or football cards waiting for my brother and me every Saturday morning. The candy was tasty, but the gum inside the pack of cards wasn't very good. Still, we looked forward to Saturdays on the farm.

My parents were hard workers and provided a good life for us. However, they started a family early in life and I know that was challenging. I was an unplanned pregnancy, yet they made the decision to get married and start a life together. Neither of them went to college, because they had kids so young. They made the best of it, but I know they were proud of me for doing things a bit differently in my life. My mom eventually went to stenographer school but never pursued a job in this field. I remember playing with her stenograph machine when I was young. My parents are wonderful people who gave my brother and me a great childhood.

My maternal grandfather, Jim Fods, was very special to me. I always loved getting some "tractor time" with him on his White 2-105 tractor. A generous, giving family man, Grandpa Fods was famous for giving birthday spankings. He was always enthusiastic, but without fail he lost count *every time*. He was also a very fast driver. We used to yell "Cop!" to get him to slow down. He knew there wasn't a police officer nearby, but he played our game to humor us. He was well-respected by every-one in his community and adored by his family. He used to slip a $100 bill to my mom and dad whenever we left on a family vacation, saying, "Dinner is on me."

On Grandpa and Grandma Fods' farm, a path ran through the grove, and we did countless laps on a Kawasaki three-wheeler. We drove fast, and my favorite part was careen-ing around the corners as fast as I could go. Sometimes I got the occasional branch in the face, which wasn't pleasant.

It seemed that Grandpa Fods could fix anything. He always tinkered in his shop, coming up with creative ways to fix machinery and other odds and ends. I'm sure that helped him be one of the few farmers who survived the farming crisis of the early 1980s. Every farmer struggled during that time and many of them didn't make it, but Grandpa Fods did. He knew farming was a cyclical business, and there would be good and bad years.

He was known for saying that "the wagon wheel is going to come back around." I found this to be true in my career, because the stock market, good deeds, etc., always came back around.

Every year, our family made an annual trek to the South Dakota State Fair. Rick Crittenden, a neighbor who carpooled with my dad to and from Gehl Manufacturing, always gave us money for unlimited rides at the fair. We kids had a blast! I remember having such fun on a ride that spins in circles, listening to "Pour Some Sugar on Me." We also stopped in Forestburg and bought watermelons on the way home.

Every few Sundays, we went to see my great-grandparents, Grandma Leona's parents, in Edgerton, Minnesota. Their names were Ed and Myrtle Baartman. The staple snack was round cinnamon bread with Cheez Whiz spread over the top and Squirt soda. We played pool in their basement, but TV was not allowed. Edgerton was a Dutch Reformed community, and they didn't watch TV on Sundays. In Edgerton, the only place to buy alcohol was at the bowling alley.

Great-Grandpa and Great-Grandma Baartman always traveled during the summers in their white and green Winnebago camper. I remember fishing with Great-Grandpa on the bridge by my paternal grandparents' house, west of Chester, and catching northern fish. The story and size of the fish grew over time!

Grandpa and Grandma Fods were generous people. Every year, they made an annual Christmas pilgrimage to Sioux Falls and shopped for presents. They loaded all the gifts in the back of their pickup and drove the whole load to the family Christmas party. There were over forty people in the family, and they bought gifts for everyone. The pickup was filled to the brim, and we all lined up, squirming with excitement, as we waited for our gift to be unloaded from the back. Generosity was baked into everything my grandparents did. For example, they faithfully cared for the local church cemetery for forty-six years. We often mowed it as a family—Grandpa Fods, Grandma Fods, my uncles, my aunt, and my brother. Grandma Fods always made a picnic, which we ate at the cemetery. It usually included a Braunschweiger sandwich, a Snickers candy bar, and a Squirt pop. Grandpa Fods smoked Camel cigarettes like a chimney, so he'd mow and smoke.

Grandpa Fods gave me wonderful memories, but the *most important* thing he taught me was how to treat other people. He was a living example of generosity and made everyone feel as if they were the only person in the room. He was an expert at making people feel special, valued, and loved.

Grandma Leona Fods was also a wonderful lady. As of this book's publication, she's still living. Her mom (my great-grandma) lived to be ninety-six so the longevity genes are strong on that side of the family.

My great-great grandma's name was Tunie Kreun, and I recall attending her one-hundredth birthday party. She died shortly thereafter. My strongest memory of Grandma Fods is when she cut my hair as a young boy. I loved it when she blew on my face to get the hair off, because she chewed Big Red cinnamon gum.

My Grandpa Schut was a really good guy, too. He was pretty quiet, smoked a pipe, and *always* wore Key bib overalls and Air Jordan basketball shoes. He smoked nothing but Carter Hall tobacco and was never without a set of matches in his breast pocket. On several occasions, his "strike anywhere" matches caught fire in his bibs, and he had the scars on his chest to prove it. He owned Allis-Chalmers tractors, which is why I love orange to this day. In March of 2021, I bought a 1971 190XT similar to his 1969 Allis-Chalmers 190XT.

One of my strongest memories with Grandpa Schut happened when I was at their house having supper. I didn't want to eat my peas. He looked at me and said, "You've never had to go hungry." That really stuck with me. The last time I saw Grandpa was at the hospital. I told him I loved him. His hands were so warm. There were other family members in the hospital waiting room. I was told, "Your Grandpa Merle was so poor that they used soup cans as glasses. Poor people in those days ate lard sandwiches. When your grandpa was young, he gave half of his lard sandwich to a kid who forgot their lunch." He was a good and generous man.

As mentioned earlier, Grandma Schut was famous for her Saturday morning treat bags. She was a heavy lady who *loved* cooking and baking. We had a yearly Christmas tradition of baking and decorating cookies with all the neighbor kids, and I always came home from her house with a five-gallon pail *full* of cookies. In fact, my earliest memory of Grandma Schut is her baking cookies. I also remember the Schwan's delivery man often stopping at her house. She was a major fan of good food. There was always candy hiding in a brown paper bag on top of the pantry, and she never missed a chance to have jelly beans on the table.

My childhood memories are full of days on the farm, hanging with my dad or grandpa(s) on the tractor. We'd work or play all morning, then head in for lunch with Grandma Schut. While she *loved* food, she was also famous for burning things. She'd put a goulash in the oven, the top generously sprinkled with cheese, then forget about it and burn it black. We just laughed, pulled the black stuff off the top, and ate it anyway.

At home, we ate a lot of Moose Brothers pizza, because my parents both worked two full-time jobs. Moose Brothers was a frozen pizza company that delivered to your door, and wow, did I love those things! My parents were busy, hard-working people, so meals consisted of convenient, easy-to-prepare food.

I have two younger brothers. Pat is two years younger than me, and Brad is twelve years younger. Brad and I are so far apart in age that I didn't really get to know him until we were adults. Pat and I are a different story. We truly grew up together and fought like brothers. I even threw shoes at him! Pat often chased me, but I was faster and always outran him. A few of our scuffles ended in stitches but nothing too disastrous. One of my fondest memories of Pat happened at Grandpa and Grandma Fods' house. I didn't eat all of my hotdog at lunchtime, so Grandpa Fods put the hotdog in my pocket, and Pat took it out and ate it!

Our family was the last to get a VCR, at least in my class, but we were the first ones to get a CD player. I was in sixth grade and still vividly remember it—a Fischer stereo system that we bought from Lakebrook TV & Appliance in Madison. The speakers were enormous! The first CDs I bought were "Tiffany" and the "California Raisins." That stereo gave us a lot of great memories.

My favorite childhood holiday was Christmas. As an adult, it's Thanksgiving, but as a kid, nothing was better than opening presents under the tree on Christmas morning. My strongest Christmas memory is the year Pat and I got black Huffy bicycles. My parents stayed up late putting them together the night before and had them sitting in front of the tree on Christmas morning. It was the first time we had new bikes, and we were so excited that we went outside and rode them in the snow. I also loved getting toy tractors as Christmas presents, and I still have several of them today.

On Saturday, November 24, 2018, we invited Grandpa and Grandma Fods to our place for ribs and all the fixings. It was a regular night, with them departing around 9 p.m. (they rode with my parents). Justin (Jen's brother) was out tilling the fields at 2 a.m. to try to beat the weather. My dad knew he was in the field in front of our house. My mom called us numerous times, but we had our phones on silent and didn't answer. Justin came knocking on the front door and said something was wrong with my grandpa and we needed to head to the hospital immediately. I looked at the chair he had just sat in only five hours earlier and thought, "Is this the end?" Jen drove because I was on the phone with my mom. When we arrived at the hospital, Grandpa was unresponsive. I told him I loved him, and he was gone by noon the next day. Thankfully, Grandpa had his last supper with my family and me.

## TEN THINGS I LEARNED FROM MOM

I created this list because I wanted to capture the important lessons I've learned from my mom. She always said, "Do as I say, not as I do." Though it sounds funny, I embraced her teaching on this, because I saw how hard my parents worked to provide a good life for us, and I know things would have been easier for them if they had finished their educations before starting a family. I attribute much of my success to listening to Mom and "doing as she said, not as she did." I went to college, got my degree, started my career, then had a family. Her advice on this has always stayed with me. Both of my parents modeled generosity and showed us the right way to treat people.

1) Pastors are people, too.
   a) As a church secretary, Mom worked regularly with pastors. She also worked closely with professors during her time at DSU. I feel her advice on this groomed me to be comfortable approaching leaders. I was exposed to pastors and professors from an early age, so I was never afraid to approach someone in a place of authority or leadership. Mom showed me that they are people, too.
2) Never miss a chance to use the restroom.
   a) This one is what it is! I've had a small bladder since childhood, and Mom emphasized I should *never* miss a chance to use the bathroom. This particular advice came after a fourth-grade teacher refused to let me use the restroom during class.
3) The bigger they are, the harder they fall.
   a) I believe this advice applies to anyone who is haughty or thinks too much of themselves. When they fall, they fall hard. The opposite of haughtiness is humility, and I place a lot of importance on being humble.
4) Give more than you receive.
   a) My parents were always giving. I believe Mom learned this from her dad, my Grandpa Fods. She is the embodiment of a go-giver.
5) It's easier to smile.
   a) We all have a choice to make each day. Will we choose to have a good day or a bad day? Mom taught me it's always easier to smile and have a good attitude.

6) Wash your own clothes.
   a) This lesson speaks to being responsible for oneself. Mom had us washing our own clothes and cooking meals around age ten. I'm thankful she showed us these skills and taught us how to be responsible and self-reliant.
7) Kill 'em with kindness.
   a) Even if you don't care for someone, it doesn't give you a license to be mean or inconsiderate. Make the choice to treat them well, because the way you treat people says much more about you than it does about them.
8) Do things you don't like to do.
   a) She showed me how to get the unpleasant chores out of the way first. Tackle the hardest tasks during the first part of the day while you're fresh and have the most focus. Also, do things you don't want to do because it's character building. I *hated* walking beans—the hand-weeding of acres of soybeans—as a kid, but doing so was excellent training, developed my strong work ethic, and I got paid $3 an hour.
9) Everything comes in threes.
   a) I don't know why this is true, but it is! Events in life seem to happen in sets of three, especially funerals.
10) My mom always said to treat the janitors and secretaries with respect, because they can get you access to anything/anyone you want. I still remember the custodian's name at Northern State University. There were a bunch of them, but I grew particularly fond of Jake.

# CHAPTER TWO

# COMING OF AGE

## HIGH SCHOOL

My high school years were generally a very happy time of my life. I attended Chester Area School in South Dakota from 1991–1995. As I grew older, I loved playing sports. Maybe that love was cultivated through my time as the "ball boy" at DSU football games? I was a decent basketball player and played all through high school, but baseball was my best sport. I wore the #3 jersey and played second base. I played for Chester and Wentworth, and the Madison VFW team. My proudest moment was hitting an over-the-fence home run in Ramona. It was my first and last. I also played football until my freshman year, but I knew early on that I wasn't built for lots of contact.

I was five feet nine inches tall and weighed 125 pounds, so I did the next best thing—I became the team manager!

In addition to sports, I was involved in a ton of extracurricular activities like 4-H, Future Farmers of America (FFA), jazz band, swing choir, and National Honors Society. I was a busy high school kid. I credit many of my leadership skills to my time in 4-H and FFA. I was the 1995 State Ag Sales Champion for FFA. This was a judged competition in which we were interviewed, mock-sold a product (mine was work boots), and took a written test on sales. The judges told my FFA advisor that I was the only student who actually asked for the sale. I remember sitting in the auditorium listening as they read the list of winners. I was shocked when they called my name for first place. What a great feeling! That was a turning point for me; it validated my ability and made me think I could succeed at anything, as long as I prepared and worked hard. During this time, I was also on the "parliamentary procedures" team, and believe it or not, knowing "Roberts Rules of Order" has come in handy many times in my adult life! I strongly believe my school years laid a strong foundation of community involvement in my life.

My favorite class in high school was history. I'm still a huge history buff, and love reading about it and learning from it. It didn't hurt that I had a great teacher, Mr. Bass. English class came in a close second. Mr. Bohl was my English teacher, and I was one of the weird kids who actually liked writing papers.

While I loved all the sports and extracurriculars, my girlfriend, Jen, was my favorite part of high school. We had keyboarding class together, and I still can't believe she "liked" me first. The homecoming dance was on October 2, 1992, and

I was planning on asking either Jen or another girl. One of my classmates, Heather, who eventually would be the maid of honor in our wedding, told me, "I think Jen will go with you." I had her double-check, just to make sure I wouldn't get rejected. Jen said yes and the rest is history.

## MY FIRSTS

My first job, other than walking beans or throwing bales on the farm, was selling footwear at Tradehome Shoes. I *loved* that job. It was a commission-based sales position, and I made $17–18 per hour in the mid-90s, because I learned how to sell a lot of shoes.

Though I worked at Tradehome, I still helped on the farm. I loved cutting alfalfa with the windrower. It was like mowing a huge lawn with the biggest, toughest mower you can imagine. The only downfall was the rough ground in the field made my CDs skip so I resorted to "dubbing" my CDs to cassettes. For anyone born after 1985, this meant playing the CD on a special machine, which then transferred the music to a recordable cassette.

Cultivating fields on the 3010 John Deere was also a favorite chore. There was no cab on the tractor, and the seat sagged to the right, because Grandpa Schut always leaned to the right, smoking his pipe and carefully avoiding the rows of young crops as he drove. In fact, the paint was worn off the fender where his forearm rested. As I pulled the six-row cultivator across the field, I did the same thing, leaning over and watching the chain hanging from the front axle, ensuring

I stayed on track and didn't dig up the newly sprouted corn or beans. The front end of the tractor wasn't heavy enough for the cultivator, so if I let the clutch out too fast the tractor popped a wheelie. I also helped out by hauling grain during harvest season. We had straight trucks, not semis with trailers, and we hauled our loads to the grain elevator in Chester, which is no longer there—it was destroyed by a tornado on August 9, 1992.

My first vehicle was a blue 1984 Ford LTD with a 5.0-liter, 302 engine. The craziest memory I have of that vehicle happened when my brother, Pat, and I pulled out on the driveway, just as a big, farm service truck drove by and ran over the hood like wheels on a monster truck. As you can imagine, our eyes were huge!

I graduated high school in 1995 with a class of twenty-four students. Fun fact: Jen graduated in 1996 and *also* had twenty-four kids in her class. Graduation was a big deal to me for many reasons. In fact, I only threw away my high school graduation cards in the summer of 2021. My Grandma Schut passed away just over a year before I finished high school; after the ceremony, I went to the cemetery and put my lapel flower on her grave. Then I went to Taopi Hall in Colton, South Dakota, for a joint graduation party with my Aunt Julie Fods (who was the same age as me) and my cousin, Ryan Fods.

After graduating high school, I attended college at Northern State University in Aberdeen, South Dakota. I was the first member of my family to attend a four-year university, and I had doubts about whether I could make it or not. Winning the FFA sales competition was a big confidence booster, and it gave me the courage to pursue my college degree. I certainly made the most of my time at Northern. By graduation, I knew nearly everyone on campus by name. I also served as the student body president. My time at Northern cemented in those high school lessons of hard work, having fun, and enjoying the experience.

# CHAPTER THREE

# MY BRIDE - JEN

## OUR FIRST DATE

My all-time favorite "first" is my first date with Jen. For the record, she liked me first. We sat next to each other in keyboarding class. I thought she was cute, and she must've thought I was cute, too, because when I asked her to be my date to the homecoming dance, she said, "Yes." We danced the night away as Guns N' Roses, Skid Row, and Warrant blared over the speakers. After the dance, I knew I wanted to go on another date with her; she was pretty, and she liked me. We officially started "going steady" on October 23, 1992.

Our courtship was fun, sweet, and young. We went to dinner and a movie in Madison on one of our first dates. After the movie, I asked if she wanted some ice cream. She said, "No thanks, I'm still full."

I replied, "There's always room for ice cream because it fills in the cracks!"

She also used to bring me Long John doughnuts from Gary's Bakery after her weekly piano lesson in Madison. Another favorite memory is when we accidentally drove down a minimum-maintenance gravel road and got very, very stuck. Before we turned onto it, I'd asked her, "Jen, do you think this road is open?"

"I think so," she replied.

Turned out it was neither open nor plowed, and I buried the car in a snowdrift. Jen was a good sport, getting out to push while I steered from inside the car. We eventually got it out and continued on our date.

## OUR COURTSHIP

When we started "going steady," we were both relatively young, so our first Christmas together was humorous. I bought her a sweater because I didn't know what else to buy. In 1994, I started working at Tradehome Shoes, and I used part of my first check to buy her perfume. I still remember the brand, *Sunflower*. We enjoyed high school together and all the whimsical, youthful memories it brought. Jen was quite good at track, and I used my excused absences to go to track meets, where I was "supporting the team"—but I was only watching Jen.

Valentine's Day at Chester Area School was a big deal. Bouquets of sweet-smelling flowers filled the office, ready for delivery to all the high school sweethearts. I made sure I bought Jen flowers every year. She went to South Dakota State University (SDSU), and I attended Northern State University (NSU). I always joke that she had thousands of guys to pick from at SDSU, and she couldn't find anyone better than me.

## MARRIAGE

Jen and I dated for six years before I proposed. At the time, she lived in a trailer house near the airport in Brookings, and I got down on one knee in her bedroom and asked her to marry me. I know, I know. Romantic (sarcasm intended), but I couldn't wait to ask her. She said, "Yes!" immediately.

After we told our families about the engagement, Grandpa Fods said, "It's about time."

Before our wedding, our pastor told us, "Marriage takes a lot of work." He was right, and I've never forgotten that advice. It does take work, but good communication goes a long way in making that work productive. In twenty-nine years, Jen and I have not had a significant disagreement or knock-down-drag-out fight of fight. It's been pretty smooth sailing, because we always communicate with each other; we work hard to stay on the same page.

The morning of July 22, 2000 dawned, clear and bright—a perfect day for a wedding! We were married at First Lutheran Church in Colton, South Dakota. Our keyboarding teacher, Tom Main, who was also Jen's track coach, said he's never attended a more organized wedding. It was a perfect day that went off without a hitch. We held the reception and dance at

Nicky's Restaurant and Lounge in Madison, serving cold cuts, pasta salad, and potato salad for the meal. Then it was off to the Black Hills of South Dakota for our honeymoon. We stayed in a mountain cabin and dined on steaks and sweet corn we brought from home. We also watched many movies (*Varsity Blues* was a favorite) and drank a lot of wine.

At the time of writing this book, we've been dating/married for twenty-nine years, and it's all been superb. We've grown our family, gone on vacations with good friends, matured as individuals, and grown as a couple. We're now navigating our biggest obstacle—my illness—but we're doing it the same way we've faced every other challenge, which is together.

One tool I want to pass on to my girls is *The Five Love Languages*. It's been a tremendous help to Jen and me as we've walked through life's highs and lows.

Jen, thank you for the beautiful life we've built together.

# CHAPTER FOUR

# GROWING A FAMILY

## STARTING A FAMILY

Our journey to starting a family began with loss then hope. We experienced two miscarriages before our eldest daughter, Makayla, was born. We didn't know it at the time, but Jen has a clotting disorder that made carrying the pregnancies to term very difficult. Despite the miscarriages, we remained hopeful that we would have children, and once the doctors figured out her diagnosis, there was a solution—giving herself a shot in the belly every day. She did this throughout her pregnancies with all three of our girls.

When we learned Jen was pregnant with Makayla, we were excited but hesitant. We hoped the shots would do their job and maintain a successful, full-term pregnancy. Thankfully, the doctors were right, and the injections worked. We attended birth classes at Avera hospital, and one night the facilitator had us go around the room and say which features we'd like our child to inherit. I said, "The dimple in my chin."

I was at a golf tournament the day Makayla was born. When I got the call that Jen had gone into labor, I was on the 17th hole. That was on a Friday. Since it was my first kid, I chose not to finish the round. Jen was actually at the hospital working when her water broke. That was around 3 p.m. on a Friday. Funny enough, that was Jen's last scheduled day of work, so Makayla came right on time! When Makayla was born on Saturday, July 15, 2006, I told Jen, "Hey, I could've finished my round of golf." She didn't find that funny. Makayla was a beautiful baby; even the nurses at the hospital commented on her beautiful complexion.

Being a new dad was scary because I didn't know what I was doing, but it was also thrilling; I had a precious little life to provide for and protect. Jen and I knew we wanted several children, so we had our babies in quick succession. All three girls were born in just three-and-a-half years.

Our second daughter, Katelyn, was born on January 15, 2008. Jen's birthday is January 14, so she spent her thirtieth birthday in labor. Katelyn's labor and delivery went pretty fast, and I recall we barely made it to the hospital in time for her to be born. Little Makayla stayed at home with her grandparents. The second row of our car quickly filled up with two car seats.

Our youngest daughter, Alyssa, arrived on February 2, 2010, and suddenly the backseat overflowed. We had a full and happy home with three girls under four.

Before we had Makayla, the birth class instructor told us, "You don't get to choose the demeanor of your kids," and that's true. Thankfully, all three of our daughters have loving, caring, easy-going personalities. They enjoy art and love to read, so academics has come quite easily for them all. I would drop the girls off at elementary school, and I'll never forget the way their little ponytails bounced back and forth as they walked into the building. I love being a girl-dad!

It means so much to Jen and me when we hear feedback from the girls' teachers about their pleasant attitudes or good grades. We saved those emails. One of my "proud dad" moments was asking the girls, "What was your favorite part about today?" as I tucked each one into bed each night. They eventually grew out of this routine, but I treasured those moments when they were young. We always tried to treat each girl as an individual, and the best parenting advice I've received was, "They're your kids. Raise them the way you want." That's the advice I pass on to my daughters and anyone else who asks. The second-best parenting advice I got is that there is no one-size-fits-all parenting style.

## OUR FIRST HOME

Jen and I purchased our first home in 2001. It was a split-level house on the east side of Sioux Falls, 111 South Hampton Avenue. It was a victory for us to purchase our first home, because up to that point my parents had never owned a home, and they didn't purchase their first house until ten years after we bought ours. Much like going to college and earning my four-year degree, buying our first home was an important goal and milestone in my life. We lived there for four years. In the process, we fixed up the house, finished the basement, and sold it for a profit. We lived at our next house, 809 W. Quail Creek Cr., for sixteen years, and that's the home we lived in when our girls were born.

## FAVORITE FAMILY MEMORIES

Surprising the girls with a trip to Florida and Disney World is one of my favorite family memories. It was a joy watching them experience the ocean for the first time. The day we went to Disney World, one of the girls left their doughnut on top of the stroller and a squirrel came and ate it. The Disney World staff replaced it and gave us five coupons for ice cream. Now that's customer service!

Picking up our dog, Teddy, is another favorite family memory. Some folks spent $1500 on him as a Christmas present for their kids, then decided they didn't want him anymore. The Humane Society director is a friend of mine, so she called me and said, "You have to come to look at this dog." They held him for us until we could get there to pick him up, and he was so tiny they kept him with the cats. He's a teacup parti Yorkie and fully grown weighs 2.6 pounds.

Having a family is a beautiful blessing, and it's something I hope each of my girls can experience. I hope they all find guys who value them and treat them right. I hope they always refer to "Ten Things I Learned From Mom" in chapter one. I hope their spouses are the kind of men who live according to those principles.

## CAREER FOUNDATIONS

We grew our careers as we grew our family. I worked at Wells Fargo while Jen was in her pharmacy residency. After residency, she signed on with Avera as a clinical specialist for pediatrics and the NICU. With our daughters being young, that was a challenging role, and seeing babies sick or dying was devastating for her. Currently, she manages Sanford's anticoagulation clinic which mainly serves elderly patients.

Though I wanted to be a financial planner in college, Steve Sershen gave me sound advice when he said, "Tim, go get a real job first. Then pursue financial planning." Working at Wells Fargo provided me with a foundation of experience. It was also nice to have benefits and a steady paycheck as we started and grew our family. I started in the collections department; then, I got promoted to the credit underwriting department. I did that for one year then became a business development analyst. In this job, I trained the bank branches on how to sell credit cards. After that, I became the manager of the inbound call center. I managed about twenty college students and two older ladies who answered phones. I called the more senior gals my "mother hens." They watched over everyone.

In the early 2000s, I reached a point where I knew the time had come to pursue my passion for financial planning. While at Wells Fargo, I studied for my securities and insurance licenses. After I passed my tests, I resigned in March of 2003 and went to work for Waddell & Reed, where I stayed until 2010.

Dad holding me

Five Generations – Tim, Pam Schut, Leona Fods,
Myrtle Baartman and Tunie Kreun

My great, great grandma, Tunie Kruen, holding me

Me holding Curious George

All bundled up

Me at four months old

Me and my mom

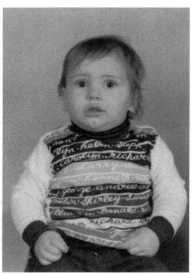
Me at one year old

Carving pumpkins

Smoking Grandpa Merle Schut's pipe

My first haircut at Grandma Fods'

Talking on the phone

Me at two years old

My second birthday

Me and my brother, Pat

Grandma Marlene Schut reading me a book

Tim, age five and Pat, age three

Kindergarten, age six

Me riding the Kawasaki three-wheeler

First day of school

Decorating cakes – Pat German did an article on us for the Madison *Daily Leader*

Our family, Tim, age thirteen, Pat, age eleven, Brad, age nine and half months, Pam, age thirty-one, Dale, age thirty-three

Our family, winter of 1991

Moving Tamara to Nashville, TN. Grandpa Merle Schut,
Dale Schut, Pat, Tim and Brad

Family pic

Tim, Brad, and Pat

Tim, Jen, and Kari (Fods) Dossett - 1995

Tim playing trombone in the marching band

Christmas – I got an NSU sweatshirt!

Jen and Tim at Prom, 1994

Senior pics

Senior pics

Senior pics

Senior pics

Senior pics

Jen and Tim – senior pics

High school graduation!
Mom putting my
corsage on me

High school graduation at Taopi Hall

Jen's senior prom

CHESTER HIGH SCHOOL
1995 - 1996

Jen's senior prom

Pat's prom

47

Graceland

Front: Jen Baumberger, Heather Hanson, Deanna Brown
Back: Tim Schut, Tom Siemonsma, Scott Backus

College graduation with my parents

College graduation with Jen

My birthday at our first house

Dad's leisure suit that he wore for his wedding

Our wedding, July 22, 2000

Tim, Jen, Grandma Leona Fods, and Grandpa Jim Fods

Tim and Jen in 2013

Family pic, 2013

Family pic, 2015

Mount Rushmore, 2015

Nashville, 2017

July 4, 2020

Thanksgiving, 2020

# CHAPTER FIVE

# SUCCESS PRINCIPLES

## SUCCESS DEFINED

I can sum up my definition of success in three words: integrity, humility, and drive. I chose integrity, because you can't have true, lasting success in business if you lack integrity. It means being truthful, transparent, and living with character. I chose humility because, as my mom always said, "The bigger they are, the harder they fall." All the great leaders I look up to are humble. Dave Rozenboom is an excellent example of this. I worked closely with Dave for five-and-a-half years, and he's as good as the day is long. He leads with humility. Finally, I chose the word "drive" because work ethic indicates future success. From the time I was a young boy, I wanted to do my best at everything. I strongly dislike lazy people, and I don't have patience for "push types" who aren't self-motivated. Being self-propelled is crucial.

One of my favorite methods of measuring life success is setting defined, specific goals. I develop personal, professional, family, and health goals each year. My personal goals are usually simple things, like reading a certain number of books each year to help me grow and mature as a person. As a family, we love setting our goals during Christmas break. For instance, we select a campfire goal for how many family campfires we want to have together each year. In 2021, we had a goal of having ten, and I think we had seven of them.

I have two specific days each year where I invest time in setting my goals. It's usually the first Thursday and Friday of December. I pick my one word to be my theme for the year and set goals in each of my four crucial categories. My spiritual goals include going to church when we're in town and giving back to my community. I see involvement in my community as part of my ministry and worship.

## SUCCESS PHILOSOPHY

There are a few core values and beliefs that I believe have made me successful. Relationships are one of those keys, and they're never going out of style. Even in today's culture, where most things are bought online with zero human contact, you still need relationships. Solid relationships are the foundation of the business world, and fostering key relationships has contributed to my career success more than any other factor. The adage still rings true that "it's not what you know, it's who you know." Relationships are the foundation of success.

The second key to success in my career is growth and learning. I strive to get better every day. As I mentioned earlier, I don't like lazy people, and I identify with hungry, growth-focused people much better. You can cultivate a growth mindset through reading books, attending seminars, studying for new licenses and skills, and listening to audiobooks and podcasts.

A critical book that cemented my growth and generosity mindset is *The Go-Giver*. Two people in one week suggested I read it, and when that happens, I take the recommendation seriously. I bought the book and immediately began putting the principles to use. One of the key ideas in the book is "stop keeping score." At the time, I was sending a colleague quite a bit of business, but he hadn't returned the favor. Truthfully, I was a tad frustrated with him. Then I read *The Go-Giver,* and I thought, "I need to send him this book and expect nothing in return." I sent him a copy with a note written inside that said, "Read this book and then let's go to lunch to discuss it."

He called me by 9:30 p.m. that night and said he'd read it in its entirety. We scheduled lunch for later that week, and he told me, "This book is going to change the way I do business." He ordered one hundred copies of the book and wrote on the inside cover of each book, "If you'd like to meet my Gus, I'd love to introduce you to him." Over the next three years, he introduced many people to me over lunch or coffee. A few years later, during an interview at a Sioux Falls Sales and Marketing Executives event, Craig Lloyd was asked what books he'd read recently. I smiled when he said, "*The Go-Giver*, and I loved it." I knew my friend had given it to his daughter, who'd given it to Craig.

My third core value is fun. It's important to enjoy every day to its utmost, and you need to have fun and enjoy what you're doing. Going back to Mom's list of ten rules to live by, smiling is better, and it's easier to choose to be happy.

The fourth value is giving. Even before reading *The Go-Giver,* I believed in the power of giving. We can provide from three personal wells: our time, talents, and treasure. I have given much of my time to nonprofits and worthy causes.

The fifth core value is positivity. It's much easier to be positive rather than negative. I feel sorry for chronically negative people, because that's a cumbersome burden to bear, and it's exhausting being negative or holding grudges.

My sixth and final core value is integrity. It's the foundation of truth and loyalty in relationships, and you can't have high-quality relationships without it.

## MY ONE-WORD STRATEGY

I adopted the idea of choosing one word for each year when I read the book *One Word That Will Change Your Life* by Jon Gordan. My long-time friend, Donavan DeBoer, gave me the book in 2013, and since then, I've chosen one word as a theme for each year. Somehow the word always fits perfectly. My 2021 word was "courage." I didn't realize when I chose it how appropriate it would be for my diagnosis.

Doing this for the past eight years, I've experienced how much intentionality my chosen word puts into my year. It creates a foundation of focus and purpose for the next 365 days. I think bigger and execute better based on my one word. I believe this happens because it prevents me from getting distracted and informs how I set my goals.

I began setting goals in 2005, but I was less focused and less successful at accomplishing my plans before implementing my one word. Here are the words I've chosen since implementing the one-word strategy in 2013.

- 2013: Growth
- 2014: Opportunity
- 2015: Better
- 2016: Compartmentalize
- 2017: Intentional
- 2018: Focus
- 2019: Me
- 2020: Gratitude
- 2021: Courage
- 2022: Optimism

Gratitude stands out as an important word choice. That was my word for 2020, and I was at a point in life where I needed to be a more thankful, grateful person. I was living a good, solid life, but I needed to be more aware of what I already had. Courage also stands out, because of the heavy weight of all that happened in 2021. It was a life-changing year that completely shifted my focus for the remainder of my life. Courage defines how I tackle this diagnosis head-on by talking about it openly and creating awareness for others with the same condition. I've resolved to choose a positive attitude toward this diagnosis. I'm not hiding from it or avoiding it. I'll tell my story for as long as I can to help others going through similar obstacles. One of my new favorite quotes says, "Adversity reveals a man to himself." I'm choosing the way I handle this curveball of life.

# MY GOAL-SETTING PROCESS

In 2005, I listened to Brian Tracy's audiobook, *Goals: How To Get Everything You Want Faster Than You Thought Possible*. After learning about Tracy's specific goal-setting process, I got intentional with my goals. I wish I'd started goal setting and journaling a long time ago, but I've made it a regular habit for the past sixteen years. As I've mentioned, in 2005, I began setting aside two days each year (always the first Thursday and Friday of December) to set my goals. Every year, I complete this process using four key steps.

## Step One: Brainstorming

I ask myself questions like, "What can I do this year to set myself up for success in my four key areas? As a reminder, these four areas are personal, professional, family, and health. I write all my potential goals on post-it notes and spread them out throughout my office.

## Step Two: Sorting

I sort through every post-it and evaluate the proposed goal. I narrowed my potential goals from fifty or sixty ideas written on post-its to around thirty goals.

## Step Three: Organizing

Next, I organize my goals by transferring them from post-it notes to a typed document on my computer. I aim to have six to eight goals in each of the four categories, as I find that anything more than eight per category is too overwhelming.

## Step Four: Lamination

Once I've organized my goals into their categories, I print off the finalized list and laminate it. I want them to be tough and sturdy to last throughout the year. I read them consistently, so they remain top-of-mind.

I'm aware of the goal-setting trend, which suggests setting just three to four goals. However, I haven't embraced this idea. I believe pairing my one-word for the year with my organized goals gives me the intentionality and focus needed to accomplish more than three or four things each year.

Brian Tracy once said, "You'll accomplish two-thirds of your goals within six months." I've found this to be accurate, especially when you keep your goals top of mind. I designed a custom book that I carry with me every day that contains my goals and my "daily eight." My daily eight are the eight things I want to accomplish that day. I also carry my ninety-day goals in this book. I look at these goals every day and use the Stephen Covey four-quadrant method to decide where I spend my time. These practices help me remain consistent, focused, and deliberate every day.

Success doesn't happen by accident. It requires effort, positivity, and discipline. I want my family and friends to know that if you don't have a target, you don't know where you're going. Without a purpose, the best-laid plans will fail. Unless you make a plan, you're leaving your future to chance. It's essential to have a target. If you write your goals down, you'll progress much faster in your learning curve, and you'll accomplish much more. The other thing I wish I'd started doing sooner is journaling. I regret not journaling more. I've told myself to journal consistently for the past twenty to thirty years, but I've not made it a habit yet. That's something I'm working on now.

# CHAPTER SIX

# BUSINESS AND CAREER

## MY CAREER PATH

My working life started with great experiences working on the farm. Windrowing hay—raking a row of hay to dry before being baled or stored—walking beans, picking rock—the highly untechnical yet oh-so-essential act of removing stones from a field—throwing bales, and doing other chores taught me a strong work ethic. I also worked at Tradehome Shoes during high school. However, the foundation of my professional career began at Wells Fargo Financial Bank, a subprime credit card organization. I worked there for three years and then moved into my dream career of financial planning. I knew it was time to make the shift, because I worked sixty hours per week for Wells Fargo, and I decided I'd rather work sixty hours for myself.

When I was going to college in the late 1990s, I was intrigued by the stock market. I wasn't in love with trading stocks and bonds, but the idea of financial planning and putting a long-term success plan together for clients was exciting. I moved from Wells Fargo to Waddell & Reed, working there from 2003 to 2010. I had an office in Madison, South Dakota. I spent two days per week there and three days per week in Sioux Falls. Becky Halma and I owned the building that was across the street from Wells Fargo. I enjoyed my work at Waddell & Reed, especially the long-term planning. I was always learning something new and met many great people in the process.

I felt the tides turning toward Quin Wind LLC when I heard about it from a colleague's husband. I left Waddell & Reed to join Quin Wind, but nine months later, it went defunct. I escaped unscathed from that experience, but I faced a decision. I'd left an established career at a great firm. What was next for me?

I got approved for a State Farm Insurance office, but unfortunately, the company didn't have any openings in Sioux Falls. I applied at Brookings, and they offered me Watertown, South Dakota. I didn't want to move to there, and during this time I got a call from the Investment Centers of America (ICA). They offered me a role associated with Dacotah Bank, where I was the in-house financial advisor for the four Sioux Falls area locations. I started in December of 2010 and fulfilled this role for four-and-a-half years, until August, 2015.

Reflecting back, 2010 was a pivotal year for me. I left Quin Wind because it went belly up, our daughter Alyssa was born,

I went back to Waddell & Reed, then moved to Investment Centers of America, and met Darin Ligtenberg at Farrell's eXtreme Bodyshaping. Those years at ICA were the best of my career.

Dave Rozenboom, the president of First PREMIER Bank, actively recruited me for two years before I finally agreed to leave Dacotah Bank and join his organization in August, 2015, as a financial advisor and private banker. Eventually, I was promoted to private banking manager. This role was a learning experience, and I found out I don't love managing people. I ultimately left in March 2021, because I thought my speech issues were stress-related.

This departure led me to NAI, a large commercial real estate brokerage. I started that role on June 2, and I was diagnosed on June 21, 2021. As of the writing of this book, I am enjoying my new career in commercial real estate and have officially closed on my first sale.

Though I've had a few different jobs throughout my career, a strong work ethic has always helped me succeed. I'm also a believer in working smarter, not harder. That's why I started goal setting. I realized if I worked specifically toward my target, I'd reach it much faster. I'm always willing to work hard, but I want to know that I'm working in the right direction. It's also essential to enjoy the work I'm doing. That's advice I wish to pass on to my daughters; do something you love and for which you have passion.

I think back on my early career and realize the importance of relationships. Of course, I was young and wanted to be successful, but now I know that success is impossible without deep relationships. I learned the importance of relationships early on, and I did things other young people don't usually do to maintain them. I even sent out Christmas cards while in college. My desire to foster great relationships also got me into community involvement. It's essential to know your community and the people around you.

Three of the most important lessons I've learned in my career are as follows:

1. *Be transparent.* Be honest with people and never hide anything. Tell them the truth. It always builds trust and rapport.
2. *Know and master your craft.* The only time you should be stressed is if you're unprepared or don't know what you're doing. Invest the time and resources necessary to become a master at your skill. Know your specialty inside and out. Continue reading and growing as a person and become hungry for knowledge.
3. *Invest the 10,000 hours.* The idea of taking 10,000 hours to master your craft comes from the book *The Tipping Point.* This philosophy says it takes 10,000 hours of learning and doing to master your art truly.

A few of my favorite people to follow are Tony Robbins, Brian Tracy, Jim Rohn, John Maxwell, and Bryan Dodge. It's important to have good mentors, and these guys have shared their experience with me, albeit in an indirect way.

## CAREER ACHIEVEMENTS AND LESSONS

Some of my favorite career achievements include being a top advisor at Waddell & Reed due to writing a large life case. I was at their home office in Kansas City when the stock market crashed in November 2008, and I vividly recall the way all the fund managers looked at their phones in disbelief as the market tanked.

Another career highlight was my presentation on the "Go-Giver" at the Investment Centers of America conference in Las Vegas. I won first place, beating out some tough competition.

Another high point was delivering a $1 million check to a grieving family, after helping them secure life insurance. At First PREMIER, it was an honor to get promoted to the manager of the private banking department. Now that I'm with NAI, I've secured my first few commercial listings and closed my first sale.

I don't think there are any low points; instead, I see them as learning points. As I've said, I figured out the hard way that I don't particularly appreciate managing people. My promotion to private banking manager was simultaneously a blessing and a curse. I wanted the role, but managing people was challenging. I learned I was much happier being a producer. Companies take their top producers and make them managers, which often ends in disaster. That's an important lesson I learned through personal experience.

If I were thinking about advice for my daughters, I'd want them to know it's important to ask yourself a few key questions before you accept a new job.

First, ask yourself, "Am I empowered to make the changes I want to make?" Second, consider the question, "Will I have authority over the things for which I have responsibility?" I didn't ask myself this question, and that was a mistake.

Sometimes great producers go into management roles, but they're born to produce. Your top producer isn't necessarily your best manager candidate. For example, Phil Jackson was a solid player in the NBA, but he was a legendary coach. The bottom line is that I enjoy producing and working with clients rather than managing a team. It's important to know yourself and identify and understand your skill sets and strengths.

# CHAPTER SEVEN

# COMMUNITY INVOLVEMENT

## COMMUNITY VISION

To me, community involvement means knowing the people who live around you. I believe this definition goes back to my roots. Growing up in a small town, I was involved in everything. Our tight-knit farming community supported its members through the joys and sorrows of life. Everyone brought the family a hot dish or pan of baked goods if someone passed away; that was the neighborly thing to do. I was involved in 4-H and other community groups during elementary and high school. At Northern, my involvement in campus activities steadily grew. As an adult, while working at Wells Fargo, I became involved with Junior Achievement, the United Way, and others.

I love supporting my community and I view it as part of my purpose. To me, the value of community is God's work. I know people who go to church every Sunday, and they believe this checks all the necessary boxes. However, I'm looking for something more than simple attendance. Giving back to my community is part of my spirituality. My volunteer efforts are focused on causes that support/educate children and improve my community. I love these causes, and I'm happy to give my time and talents to help them grow. Many people see volunteer work as purely an outpouring, but that's not true. It feels fantastic to give back, and volunteering enriches my life. If I hadn't volunteered, I wouldn't have met many outstanding people that I now call friends.

## COMMUNITY INVOLVEMENT HISTORY

My first board experience was through Junior Achievement in Madison, South Dakota. I volunteered in the classroom by working with kindergarteners to teach them lessons on Junior Achievement's core values: work readiness, entrepreneurship, and financial literacy. I loved working with this age group. They are fun, excited to learn, and easily bribed with candy! I also admire all kindergarten teachers, because I was exhausted after every hour in that classroom. I began as a classroom volunteer, then I became a JA board member.

Next, I moved to the Junior Achievement group in Sioux Falls. It was a similar story in that I started as a volunteer and became a board member later. This group was a much larger organization than Madison, and I enjoyed my time there. I met my mentor, Rod Carlson, while serving on this board. He's an important person in my life, and we've met every month for the past ten years for beers and wings.

I became involved with United Way during my days at Wells Fargo, and I was eventually selected to serve on Dave Rozenboom's executive cabinet. That was the first time I remember feeling like, *Wow, I'm here with the big dogs.* I thought I'd "made it," because the room was full of influential business leaders.

When working at Wells Fargo Financial, I met Brent Weiler, a bulldog when it came to community fundraising, especially at United Way. He and I became friends. Brent stayed at Wells Fargo until he was lured away by Scott Lawrence, who owned Lawrence & Schiller, and whom Brent met through United Way. Long story short, Brent died of cancer in 2014 at the age of thirty-eight. One year later, the United Way honored Brent via the Brent Weiler Bulldog Award. I received the award three years after it was established, which was a great honor, and the fact that I worked with Brent made it all the more special.

2011 was a busy and exciting year. At one point, I simultaneously served on the Junior Achievement, Young Professional's Network, Great Plains Zoo, and United Way boards. I was selected for the Great Plains Zoo executive board and helped plan their annual zoo fundraiser called the "Jungle Jubilee." I had a great time helping plan and execute that event.

# THE YOUNG PROFESSIONALS NETWORK

Perhaps my favorite community involvement story is working with the Young Professionals Network. I call this organization my "fourth child," because I'm proud of my role in helping build it. When our founding group assembled, there was no such thing as YPN in Sioux Falls, and I got involved on the ground floor, because of my involvement with Leadership Sioux Falls. I got on the steering committee to establish a YPN branch in Sioux Falls through the Sioux Falls Chamber of Commerce.

Our founding group was dynamic and motivated. We dreamed big, thought big, and executed big. We all loaded into my Suburban and traveled to Omaha, because they had a YPN branch. We attended their big annual event and thought, *We can do this in Sioux Falls.* I'll never forget the way we all huddled together in the hallway of the convention center, talking excitedly about the possibilities of creating this group in our city. The Sioux Falls Chamber of Commerce was very deliberate about engaging young professionals ages twenty-one to thirty-nine in the community, because, at that time, many of them were leaving the state, so keeping young talent in Sioux Falls was a top priority.

We planned for twenty-two months before launching, and our goal was to have one hundred members within a few months of the launch. We had a kickoff party where we nervously waited and thought, *Maybe no one is going to show?* We shouldn't have worried, because it was packed and the event launched the group with a bang. Soon, we had four hundred and then six hundred. Now there are over one thousand members in the group.

We held our first annual YPN Crossroads Summit in 2011. I spearheaded this idea and event, and it's rewarding to see it continue growing and thriving. We wanted to give our members access to community leaders, and this kind of summit seemed like a smart way to accomplish that goal. We planned the venue, secured the speaker, established event committees, and more. Our first summit event drew about 325 attendees. Our first speaker was Jenna Bush Hager, daughter of President George W. Bush. Jason Dorsey also spoke. We caught him on the way up in his career; he is now widely renowned as the "Generations Expert."

I aged out of the Young Professionals' Network at age thirty-nine, and now other talented people are leading the organization. I'm proud of my role in founding and growing YPN, and it gives me such joy to see it serve the community in an impactful way. I was the only one to graduate from Leadership Madison, Leadership Sioux Falls, and Leadership South Dakota, and for that I am very proud.

## ADVICE ON COMMUNITY INVOLVEMENT

I decide which organizations I want to engage with by determining if I'm passionate about the causes they support. If I'm not interested in it, I'll be a poor volunteer or board member. A board member expects to give away their time, talents, and treasure, which is a big expectation, so you need to care about the cause and believe in it wholeheartedly. A quality board member should willingly share their wisdom, network, and resources to move forward. In turn, a high-quality board should convey their expectations ahead of time. Before committing to a board, ask yourself, "Do I know the expectations of this board? Do those expectations match my workload?" Don't say "Yes" without knowing what you're taking on.

You might be wondering, *How do I get on a board?* My best answer is that you're asked to be involved in the organization by volunteering, and that's when you get on people's radar. I've had to say no to more opportunities than I've been able to say yes. Again, I believe it's essential to know your core values and what causes matter most to you. For me, it's kids and community. It doesn't fit me if the organization doesn't help those two areas. Organizations are hungry for volunteers, so start by simply volunteering if you want to get involved in your community. The board positions come after you've proven yourself to be a worthwhile volunteer and leader.

Another organization I'm proud to be a part of is the Sales & Marketing Executives of Sioux Falls. I was a guest at SME, and Bryan Dodge was the presenter. In my mind I said, *I WANT to be part of this organization!* I submitted my application but received a letter that I didn't qualify.

"What do you mean I didn't qualify?" I said.

I was an independent contractor, had an assistant, and ate what I killed. Turned out, they didn't allow the Northwestern Mutual and New York Life types. I was at Waddell & Reed at the time, so they lumped us all together. I fought it, and with the help of other advisors, they eventually changed the restrictions, so I became a member.

After two or three years, I wasn't going to the meetings and became disinterested. But when I met with Rod Carlson for our monthly mentor meeting, he said, "You aren't going to quit SME, you are going to join a committee." Rod had an SME directory in his briefcase, so we looked at the committees and I selected the recruitment committee. After the first meeting, I was asked to lead the committee. Mat Timmer and I co-chaired. Mat later died of a brain tumor just shy of his thirty-second birthday. We utilized LinkedIn at our meetings, and we propelled SME to a record number of members. Because of my performance on the recruitment committee, I was asked to join the Board of Directors. To think that just a few years ago, I was thinking about leaving SME entirely. I'm sure glad I didn't! I was ultimately asked to join the Executive Board of SME. When asked to serve as the board chair, I told the current chair, Jan Feterl, something was wrong with my speech, and I didn't think I would be very effective at leading SME. While I would've loved the opportunity, it was ultimately a wise choice to decline the role and focus on getting a health diagnosis.

I met Dave Rozenboom through United Way. Two years later, he was courting me to join First PREMIER Bank. I said no for two years, then realized it was an opportunity I should take. These boards and volunteer positions are good for business. I met many clients through these organizations. I've never regretted pouring my heart into a worthy organization, and I've never regretted meeting a new person. Everyone I've met has provided me with value in one way or another.

A few of my favorite "embarrassing" non-profit stories involved a pig and a kilt. When I had the Waddell & Reed office in Madison, we raised money for the United Way, and the person who raised the least money had to kiss a pig. We grilled burgers and hot dogs in front of the Waddell & Reed office and sold them. Guess who came in last? Yours truly! I pulled out my cherry Chapstick and put it on the pig. Then I gave the pig a huge smooch!

Another embarrassing time happened when raising funds for the Ronald McDonald House in Sioux Falls. Seven or eight guys got together for the cause by wearing kilts in front of 200 people. I came in second place and raised over $20,000!

In summary, here's my best advice for community involvement:

1. Analyze your interests. Identify your core values and align with organizations that support those values.
2. Count the cost of the commitment. Check out a meeting or two before officially committing.
3. Always be in the minutes. Speak up, make a difference, and be involved.

# CHAPTER EIGHT

# MENTORS

## THE VALUE OF MENTORSHIP

I believe there is tremendous value in having mentors. To me, a mentor is someone who knows more about a topic than you do. It doesn't necessarily need to be someone older than you, but they need to know more than you in the subject area you want to grow in. There are many reasons to have a mentor. One of the most important reasons is because it accelerates the learning curve of whatever skill you desire to master. I've found that leaders who are advanced in their skill set and excellent at what they do are usually willing to help and share their knowledge. Plus, everyone likes a paid-for cup of coffee. A mentor should be someone who has your best interests in mind, who knows what they're signing up for when they agree to mentor you, and a person who is kind and is your friend. This element of friendship is vital because synergy and mutual respect are the foundation of a positive mentor-mentee relationship.

We've described what a mentor should be. Now let's talk about what a mentor is not. They are not someone with whom you "BS" over lunch. Yes, a mentorship relationship should have an element of friendship, but that's not the arrangement's sole purpose. They should be people of high integrity because you're asking them to speak into your life and potentially change the way you live it. I've had lunch with many people I thought could be solid mentors, but then I got to know them and thought, *No way*. Vet your mentors carefully. Take your time and study their life before you agree to let them speak into yours. A mentor shouldn't constantly sympathize with you; they should hold you accountable to do what you commit to doing.

What happens when you don't bring mentors into your life? What's the downside? My mentors have helped me avoid many mistakes and "landmines" along my career path, especially Rod Carlson. His knowledge of the history of the community has helped me navigate the sometimes-choppy waters of community involvement and business relationships. Your mentor should do the same for you. A great mentor watches out for you and helps you be up-to-date on current and past events in the community, and guides you with a selfless perspective.

In summary, a mentor improves your life by:

1. Accelerating your learning curve
2. Guiding to avoid landmines
3. Providing genuine friendship and accountability

# MY MENTORS

I believe strongly in the power of mentorship because I've experienced its benefits many times in my career. I hope I've mentored and poured into other people on my journey as well. When you get to the top of the mountain, it's essential to go back down and bring someone else up the trail with you. If great mentors have poured into you, make it your mission to pay that generosity forward by pouring into someone else.

Many excellent mentors in my life have extraordinarily blessed me. I want to honor those people by naming them and sharing how they impacted my life in the following pages. It seems that every year, a particular person affects my life in a specific and memorable manner. This chapter is my attempt to honor those people.

## 2010 – Darin Ligtenberg

- When I met Darin, he owned Farrell's eXtreme Bodyshaping. The year 2010 was a turning point for me. Honestly, I was at a low point in my life because I was overweight, frustrated in my career, and wanted to feel better. The hardest part of going to the gym is signing up and going on the first day. Darin was the first person I met while signing up, and I thought, *I like this guy. He's going to help me get results.* Before I met him, I didn't know the difference between a carb and a protein, and I didn't know how they affected my body. He taught me about exercise and nutrition. I dropped forty-six pounds that year, and it changed my life. I grew in confidence, purpose, and focus. Thank you, Darin.

## 2011 – Mike Roby

- Mike coached me on accomplishing big business goals. He's also profoundly impacted my personal life. He used to live in Shakopee, Minnesota, and in 2011, I drove to Minnesota to spend time with him in person. I brought along my business goals, and after reviewing them, he asked, "Where are your personal goals?" He was the one who taught me that business and personal goals go hand-in-hand. Mike helped me bring intentionality and synergy to my business and personal life. He taught me time management, practice management, and relationship management. He helped me see what I could do better personally and professionally. He's been a critically important person in my life for the past ten years. Thank you, Mike.

## 2012 – Brian Spader

- I met Brian while working out at Farrell's. Darin Ligtenberg was Brian's brother-in-law at the time. We hit it off instantly, and our wives and daughters also became great friends. Brian and Lori own a cabin near Custer, South Dakota, and we stayed there several years ago with the kids and had a blast! One time at Jungle Jubilee (the fundraiser for the zoo) they were bidding on naming rights of a monkey. I asked Brian what he'd name the monkey if he won. His response was "Brian F***$g Spader." I still call him that to this day, and he calls me Ivan, which is my middle name. We attended many fundraisers together: Jungle Jubilee, the Kilts for Kids, Paws to Celebrate (Humane Society), and many more. He's a top-notch person and is now the president of Thompson Electric. Thank you, Brian.

## 2013 – Jim Komoszewski

- Jim's advice was crucial to the growth of my business. I remember Jim sitting by my desk at ICA/Dacotah Bank as we shared life stories and practice management tips. He's also a very talented musician. He even dedicated a song to me post-diagnosis. He was the most impactful person in my life in 2013. Thank you, Jim.

## 2014 – Tom Johnson

- Tom took the time to encourage me and speak positivity into my life. He made me a special card that said, "Tim's Success Card." On it were written all the disciplines and principles I'd woven into my life that made me successful. This card affirmed what I was doing right and significantly impacted me. Thank you, Tom.

## 2015 – Greg Myers

- I bought Greg's practice from him, and he's one of the nicest, most genuine people I've ever met. When they were downsizing their home, I bought their keyboard at an auction, and my girls played it at the "farmhouse" because there was no piano there. His wife, Jacki, is a very talented musician, and she was glad to see it go to a good home. At his retirement party, I told the crowd, "My only regret was not meeting Greg ten years ago." He's the definition of a salt-of-the-earth person, which showed in the quality of his clients in his book of business. I met many excellent people through that practice. He blessed me with both friends and clients. Thank you, Greg.

## 2016 – Mark Walstrom

- I met Mark through First Dakota Title Company. He periodically stopped to pick up paperwork at the bank where I worked. We hit it off, probably because we are similar personalities. We've had lots of great times together like the Summit League tournament, Sutton Bay, and Jackrabbits football games. He is a big Jacks fan, in fact, he serves on the board of trustees for SDSU. He's an enthusiastic and supportive friend. Thank you, Mark.

## 2017 – Rick Melmer

- I met Rick through the Rotary Club (I was a guest at Rotary), and I invited him out for lunch. That's one of the best invites I've ever extended because Rick is one of the top five most impactful people in my life. The bank hired him as a Growth Coach, and our relationship grew after that. I was in Leadership South Dakota (LSD) during 2018–2019, and Rick and his wife, Val, ran the LSD program. It was then that our relationship blossomed to what it is today. He still sends me a handwritten note every few weeks. He also set me up with a weekly men's group and has incredibly blessed my life. Thank you, Rick.

## 2018 – Jim Woster

- Jim Woster is a legend. I remember being at Grandpa and Grandma Fods' house, eating lunch and watching him do the livestock markets on KELO. I met Jim through the Stockyards Ag Experience board. We traveled to Madison together for a fundraising event and hit it off. Jim is a caring and kind guy who takes the time to call me every few months and offer encouragement and an atta-boy. I appreciate his intentionality and positive attitude. Everybody knows Jim Woster. He is a big supporter of SDSU and Avera Health. Thank you, Jim.

## 2019 – Matt Martin

- Matt is a magnetic person with a zest for life. I met Matt at the SME golf tournament via Evan Kindt, co-owner of Marv's Body Shop. Matt runs an American Family Insurance office in Sioux Falls. He is a one-of-a-kind guy and a really good basketball player. I've greatly enjoyed my friendship with him. Thank you, Matt.

## 2020 – Chris Mello/Nicole Zacher

- A buddy of mine, Chad Hatch, put a post on Facebook saying ever since he joined CPM Fitness, he no longer had back pain. I took a screenshot of it and two weeks later I bulged two discs in my back. I called Chad and asked, "What's with this CPM program?" CPM doesn't let anybody in; they interview you first. I passed the interview and was assigned

Nicole Zacher as my trainer. Nicole was the wife of Mike Zacher, who was a classmate in Leadership South Dakota. Nicole is a trained physical therapist, which was a perfect set up for my back. I only went through the program for six months, but six months is all it took for those two to have an impact on me. They are both positive, energetic people who truly care about their clients. Thank you, Chris and Nicole.

## 2021 – Gregg Brown

- Gregg is a Managing Director at NAI Sioux Falls. He is one of the nicest guys I know. When I told Gregg about my disease, he was more than accommodating. I started at NAI June 2, 2021 and was diagnosed on June 21, 2021. So, I never really got started. Gregg showed me grace and really supported me through this disease. I met him through Marcus Mahlen (when I did Leadership South Dakota with Marcus). Gregg is the proud dad of two sons. Thank you, Gregg.

## 2022 – Lon Stroschein

- I've known Lon since college. He went to Northern State University for 2 years then transferred to South Dakota State University. Lon and I used to be neighbors when we lived on Quail Creek Circle. He worked at Raven Industries as an Executive for just over 14 years. Lon is a farm kid from Warner. Their family farm has been in the family for generations. In fact, you can still see wagon wheel tracks in the pasture. What made him the most impactful person of the year is when he volunteered to the interview with my South Dakota Public

Broadcasting Television special. It includes my story and my disease. What makes it most impactful is that my mom, dad and wife are involved in it. Thank you, Lon.

## ADDITIONAL IMPORTANT MENTORS AND FRIENDS

*Kory Davis.* Kory and I met through Wells Fargo, and we hit it off. I can't even explain how important Kory is to me. He is always there when I need him. Plus, he has the biggest Super Bowl parties at Tavern 88, the bar inside his house. From the late nights at Borrowed Bucks to all the houses he sold me, six in total, I appreciate his friendship deeply.

One of my favorite stories with Kory is when I mailed him *The Go-Giver* book. He texted me at 5:30 p.m. and said he got it in the mail. By 9:30 p.m. he'd finished it. Whenever I gift a book, I write a personal note in the Gus chapter encouraging them to reach out to me for lunch. At lunch, Kory said, "This book is going to change the way I do business." The next week he called and said, "I ordered 100 copies of *The Go Giver*, and I'm going to write in the chapter on *Gus*, 'If you ever want to meet my Gus give me a call.'" That was fantastic! Kory opened up his network for me.

Another favorite memory is when we (Kory, Jeremy DeCurtins, Chad Nekl, and I) took in a Minnesota Twins game and a Minnesota Timberwolves game on the same day. A few years after that, the four of us went to Lambeau Field for a Vikings and Packers game. Needless to say, we had a great time. Kory's friendship has blessed my life tremendously.

*Larry Young.* We worked together at Tradehome Shoes starting in 1994 and had a lot of fun selling shoes. We went to Huset's Speedway on occasion and watched the races on Sunday. Larry is one of those guys I kept in touch with throughout college. When I graduated college, I went to work for Wells Fargo Financial Bank, and Larry was working there, too. He became my boss for a second time. Larry eventually moved to Wells Fargo Commercial Lending in downtown Sioux Falls. From there, he went to Yankton where he served as Market President. He eventually moved to Arizona, where he also served as Market President. During this time, Larry and I stayed in touch. When he left Wells Fargo, he moved back to Sioux Falls and now runs his consulting business, Boiling Frog Development. We've now been friends for nearly twenty-eight years.

*Clay Wilhelm.* Clay and I met at Northern. I knew his wife, Holly, before Clay did. After college graduation, Clay went to work for Waddell & Reed in Sioux Falls. By that time, he was married to Holly. They lived next door to Jen and me in the Holly 100 apartment buildings.

Funny story, I was watching a Vikings game one day while Jen was at work. I get really into sports, and I was yelling and screaming at the TV. Clay thought there was some sort of domestic violence happening so he knocked on the door. Jen wasn't there, and I told him I was watching the Vikings game. We both had a good laugh from that one. Clay grew up on a farm near Faulkton, and for several years Clay, James Sigaty, Matt Teller, and I headed up to the farm to hunt pheasants, usually the second weekend after the opener.

*James Sigaty.* When I had the Waddell & Reed office in Madison, I cut out clippings from the Madison *Daily Leader* on new young professionals who had moved to town. I saw in the paper that James Sigaty came to Madison as a young dentist and joined a local practice. Shortly thereafter, the attorneys next door to our office had a holiday party, and James and his wife, Amanda, were there. We invited them to our house on Hampton, and our friendship grew. James eventually moved out of Madison and joined a practice in Sioux Falls, which he now owns. By that time, we moved to the house on Quail Creek and they bought a house only three blocks from us. We went on a vacation to Vegas with them, and that was a blast! They eventually got divorced, but James and Amanda remain close friends to this day.

*Donavan DeBoer.* Donavan and I met on our first day of college at Northern. Chris Kreul, my roommate with whom I also graduated high school, admired Donavan and Mitch Brooks' loft. We all hit it off right away. Donavan had a green Volkswagen Beetle, and we often cruised Aberdeen in it.

One time we got a wild hair to watch Jen play basketball in Chester, and Mitch, who is six feet four inches tall, crammed in the back seat of my 1985 Nissan Pulsar. After graduation, I was in Donavan and Michelle's wedding. Then they moved to Las Vegas for teaching jobs. Donavan called me at 4 a.m. to tell me they had a baby girl. He then went to Wood, South Dakota, and then Newell, South Dakota, where he was head girls basketball coach. Next, he moved to Rapid City Stevens where he was head coach as well. He eventually took the superintendent job in Parker where, as of this writing, he is today. Donavan is one of my very best friends.

*Paul Lems.* Paul and I met on January 3, 2000. We were recent college grads and new employees starting out our careers at Wells Fargo Financial Bank. A bunch of us newbies stood freezing in the foyer because you had to have a badge to enter the building, and Paul and I hit it off immediately. He and his wife, Mollie, have three girls similar in age to our daughters so there's a common synergy.

One time, while vacationing with the Lems in Hawaii, Jen and I had a little too much wine and accidentally ordered a carpet cleaner on QVC. When we got back from Hawaii, there was a box at the front door. *"What's that?"* we wondered, and then remembered, we ordered a carpet cleaner. Paul has become a great friend and we still talk weekly.

*Jeremy DeCurtins.* I've known Jeremy since we were young. We even played Little League against one another. I remember the Trojan/Bulldog basketball camps, and Jeremy was a lot better player than I was. He was even a wide receiver with the University of Sioux Falls, and they won a national championship in 1996. Jeremy completed his internship with the Sioux Falls Skyforce, and he is still there as of this writing as Vice President/General Manager. As adults, we played pickup basketball together at the empty Sioux Falls arena. He even helped put siding on our farmhouse. He's a great guy and a cheerful friend.

*Rod Carlson.* Rod has been a mentor for ten plus years. We connected through Junior Achievement in Sioux Falls, and we've met on the first Monday of every month for the past ten years. He's undoubtedly accelerated my learning curve in community involvement and helped me avoid severe landmines in the process. He also taught me the "triangle" theory of life management. This triangle consists of three points: community, personal life, and career, and it's constantly evolving and changing. It's a rotation of priorities that flex and move, which is good. That balance and shift are natural; however, you always want your personal life at the top. Once it's not, the triangle needs to be adjusted. I've always kept this triangle in mind.

I hope my daughters find mentors that positively impact their lives, like my mentors have affected mine. Mentorship is an invaluable and vital part of growing into a productive, community-minded person.

# CHAPTER NINE

# A MESSAGE TO MY FAMILY

## TO THE LOVE OF MY LIFE, JEN

You are the most perfect person in the world. Jen, I could go on and on about all the things I love about you. You are the kindest person I've ever been around. You're always positive. You're a beauty inside and out. I loved watching you play sports in high school. I'll never forget wearing my brand-new Birkenstock sandals to your track meet and burning my feet terribly. That's a funny memory.

I also loved when we were freshly married with no kids, and we went to Applebee's each week for half-price apps and drinks after 9 p.m. We always ordered Killian's Irish Red and onion peels. We've been together nearly thirty years, and we have many great stories.

Jen, I've never met anyone as kind as you. You're perfect for me. I love how smart you are. How relaxed you are. How much I enjoy you. There's no drama in our relationship. In twenty-nine years of being together, I can't remember having a significant argument. It's been smooth sailing and so good. I can't ask for a better wife. I loved watching you become a mom. I always knew you'd be a fantastic mother.

One of our first dates holds one of my favorite moments with you. I took you out for dinner and a movie, and after the movie, I said, "Let's get some ice cream." You said you were full, and I said, "There's always room for ice cream because it fills in the cracks." There are so many memorable moments it's challenging to list them all. I loved when we went to Mexico with Jason and Danielle. Vegas with Justin and Jenna was so much fun.

I remember when you left my house in high school. You always buckled up, but on this day, you didn't. You hit loose gravel and rolled your pickup. You were ejected, and Larry and Charlene found you wandering around. You were not seriously hurt, and the only proof of the accident is the scars on your leg and back.

You are the most perfect, kind person I have ever met. I love your sweet nature and curly hair. We were high school sweethearts, and that makes our relationship unique. People often say there were ups and downs in their marriage, but you and I have always had ups.

## TO MY DEAR MAKAYLA

Ever since you were born, you've had the most beautiful eyes and complexion. We have the same dimple in our chins. Your name was derived from Grandma Pam's middle name, which is Kay, and Grandma Arla's middle name, which is Jean.

Remember that special song I used to sing to you? 'I know a girl, her name is Makaya, she's real pretty, wouldn't you say-a, I know a girl, her name is Makaya, and I love her everyday. Of my three daughters, you and I are most similar. I'll never forget when you were so excited to start kindergarten that you threw up on your first day. I picked you up from school, then we cuddled and watched "Rango."

You always hold yourself to high standards and are organized, articulate, and an excellent student. I'm so excited to see what you do when you grow up. You always make me proud, but I was incredibly proud when the Washington Pavilion chose your artwork to display at their art show. I always laugh when I think of "Mommy, Daddy, Mommy, Daddy ... milk!"

I hope you always remember how much I love you and how I strove to put our family first. I want you to grow up and find a very fulfilling career. Meet a kind, caring husband and raise a great family. I am incredibly proud of the young woman you've become.

## TO MY DEAR KATELYN

You've always been my cuddler. You're shy, but once people get to know you, the real Katelyn comes out. You're funny, kind, sweet, and caring, and those dimples in your cheeks are the best. You're smart and intelligent. I can't wait to see what you do when you grow up.

I'm always proud of you, but I was particularly proud when you scored nine of your team's thirty points in your first-ever basketball game. Do you remember when you won the art contest at the public library? That was awesome. You are creative, talented, and never afraid to try new things. Since you were little, you'd sing and dance to music. I love that you still do this today. Your name is derived from your mom's middle name, Lynn, and Great-Grandma Annabelle's middle name, Grace.

I hope you grow up to have a fulfilling, meaningful career and that you meet a kind, caring husband who loves you, and together you two raise a great family. I hope you always remember how much I love you and how I put our family first.

## TO MY DEAR ALYSSA

You are always full of energy! You are also a great student, and I'm excited to see what you do when you grow up. I am always proud of you, but I was especially proud when you made cupcakes for your fourth-grade teachers. In fifth grade, you and your friend made ornaments for all the teachers.

Do you know why I love your kisses, Alyssa? "Because they're the best kisses on the whole wild world." You have always been a spirited, go-get-'em girl. You are fearless and don't ever change that. I enjoy watching you play sports. I am very proud of you! The first time you saw the ocean is a moment

I'll never forget. You were so excited! You're brave and fearless, with energy to spare.

Your name was derived from Alyssa Milano. I had a crush on her as a boy, and it doesn't hurt that there is an L, A, and Y in your name, just like your sisters. Your middle name came from your Great-Grandma, Marlene Mae Schut.

I'll never forget when we first got our dog, Teddy, and you chased him around the living room and fell into his "playpen" kennel. I have a video of it, and it's the funniest thing ever. In the winter of 2021, I pulled you and Makayla on the sled, and you fell out, but I didn't realize until I was a half-mile down the field. A funny memory! I hope you have a very fulfilling career, meet a kind, caring husband, and raise a great family. Always remember how much I love you and put our family first.

## TO MY DAUGHTERS

I had the best time with all three of you girls, from our trips to Florida to doing wood projects in the farmhouse basement and eventually the shed. I loved our family nights, watching "Heartland", "Supergirl", "Manifest", and many other shows and movies while eating Mom's homemade popcorn. Do you remember the sled rides at Grandpa and Grandma Baumberger's? Those are memories I'll always treasure. Even simple things like having dinner as a family made my day. All three of you are very intelligent. People have always complimented your mom and me on how well you carry on conversations with adults. That makes us very proud!

As little girls, I held you as much as possible. Those are memories I'll never forget. I'll always love our countless Ranger rides and campfires. When we owned a cabin in the Hills, we played pool and shuffleboard all by ourselves in the clubhouse. The Fourth of July will always hold special memories like going to Justin's, lighting fireworks, watching fireworks over the lake, and eating Grandma's homemade popcorn.

I still laugh when I remember our trip to Disney. At Animal Kingdom, we parked the stroller, then set a donut on top of the stroller and a squirrel ate it! We didn't realize it was gone until the Disney staff came up to us and offered us five coupons for ice cream.

When we lived in Sioux Falls, you played with Karis and Kiera all the time. Alisha Auen kid-sat you for four summers, and I'm grateful for the memories you made with her, like macaroons, parks, going to the swimming pool, and many more. Do you remember bedtime when I asked you, "What was your favorite part about today?" I hope you do. It was the highlight of my day. Do you remember singing "Wagon Wheel" and "Goodbye Earl"? Such fun! My most recent memory is taking the three of you to state volleyball in Rapid City. We had a blast! I love you more than words can ever fully express. You are my greatest accomplishment and my highest legacy. I love you.

**Jenna** – The real question is how do I begin to pick just one memory. I have so many fond memories, it's difficult to pick you just one. From the many wonderful meals with your smoked pork, to Fourth of July shenanigans, to wood-working afternoons. One of my first memories of you, and the one that came to mind first when you asked us to send one, is the first time I met you. Justin and I came to your house in Sioux

Falls to meet baby Katelyn. I was nervous as I was meeting the boyfriend's family. However, I instantly felt relaxed and comfortable as soon as you greeted us at the door. I remember you being so welcoming, happy, and easy to talk to. You sure helped calm my nerves, and I will always be thankful for that!

**Tamara** – This is still so vivid today. You must have been around eight or nine months old, Grandma Marlene would babysit you. I would come home from school, and you would be sitting in your Teterbabe. You had fat little legs and chubby cheeks, and lots of brown hair. I would come into the dining room and you would see me. Your whole face would light up, drool running down your face, and your little legs would jump up and down, making the Teterbabe jump crazily. Great thing to come home to!

Two memories that remind me of what an extraordinary nephew I have:

Your high school graduation—I remember you were late to your own party. You took the time to go to Grandma Marlene's grave and leave your boutonniere on her headstone. It showed me just how much she meant to you and that you would never forget her.

The second is of you speaking at Grandpa Merle's funeral. All the great stories of your time spent with him, especially the trip back from Tennessee. The pipe … and of course, his tractor seat leaning to one side, I believe due to again to him smoking that pipe? You have always been an amazing storyteller. One last story. You must have been two or three years old. I had an old sink and cabinet behind the house that I used for a playhouse, when I was younger. I took you out there to play and we made mud pies. You ended up head to toe in mud, and your grandma was not happy as I took you into the house to show her. She made me strip you out in the yard, and she sure giggled at the sight of you covered in mud!

## SPECIAL MEMORIES FROM TIM'S MOM

I remember your first Christmas! It was amazing. You were so little, but so darn cute in a little red and white snowsuit. You had a matching red/white cap. Our little Santa! You were the best Christmas present. We had so many Christmases to attend between both sides of the family and *everyone* wanted to hold you. Once we got in the door, someone would take you from us, get you out of your snowsuit, and then off you went into the festivities. We never had to worry about feeding you, changing your diaper, rocking you to sleep, for the entire party! I'll never forget the pride and joy I felt carrying you in to meet so many family members on your first Christmas!

When you were a couple years old, we took a quick trip to the Black Hills. You were so homesick for Julie that you wouldn't eat or sleep. You just kept asking for and looking for Julie. You wanted her and nothing else!

So, we decided to come home a couple days early. We got home and went straight to Grandpa and Grandma's house. so you could see Julie. Once you got to their house you (and Julie) ran in circles around the kitchen and through the dining room, so excited to see each other! You both ran in circles for a long time and you just kept saying, "Julie! Julie! Julie!" Gpa, Gma, your dad, and I just sat at the kitchen table and laughed at you two. Julie missed you much as you missed her!

I knew you would have a love for music at an early age. When we were living on the Severson place on Highway 19, we managed to find money to buy a small stereo system—record player, radio, 8-track player (I think, maybe cassette?) and small speakers!

It was set up in the corner of our dining room at a level you could reach. You were so little but somehow learned to put on your favorite music and would stand there, microphone in hand, pretending to sing along. You sang and danced, whether you knew all the words or not! Amazingly, you liked all the music we did.

I'll verify with Dad, but you don't know how long we debated at the store to figure out if we could afford that tabletop system and where we'd find the money. I think it cost around $200 but was a huge purchase for us! Remember, we only spent $500 on all three of our engagement/wedding rings, so spending this much on something fun for the house was a big deal!

***We were moving up to purchasing fun stuff as we'd already upgraded our little nine-inch TV, which was all we owned for quite a while after we got married. It sat on a cheap metal bookcase at the foot of our bed; at that time, we didn't have living room furniture, we couldn't have seen it across the room if we did! (We lived across from Jackie's then.) Great memories!

Another fun memory is getting the entire family together to surprise you at NSU when you were Student Body President. We surprised you by attending your first class of the morning! Your friends and professor knew we were all coming. Thank goodness you made it to class, because you'd had a late night partying the night before. Later, surprising you with a small reception for your outgoing and incoming student body officers was memorable. Then later that day, taking Grandpa and Grandma Fods to the Zoo Bar was great fun! That was a great time, and great memories were made. I doubt many other NSU student body presidents have had that experience.

I remember the fun times taking you and Pat shopping for school outfits to use for 4-H projects. You two would plan where you wanted to find the best outfit for the best value so you would get a purple ribbon! It was fun watching you two try on clothes and put your outfits together. Once home, we would go to the church and stand by the evergreen trees for the perfect background to take your pictures wearing your new outfits, to attach to your 4-H entry. You two always had such big smiles with your chosen outfits! Since you picked them out, I knew you'd wear them. That was the first time I realized that the in-thing was to "peg" your pant legs and the rage was to dress like Don Johnson of Miami Vice. You boys managed to pull it all off looking spectacular and getting purple ribbons! You were a fashionista at an early age!

I remember lots of trips, walking in the cold to the church with you and Pat to practice piano lessons—in a cold parish hall. It's amazing how often we'd go over to practice when we didn't have a piano at home.

I remember taking you to piano contests. You would be so nervous, but you always came home with a #1 rating. You always loved music.

An interesting tidbit. Once we got a piano in the house and didn't have to go to the church every day to practice, we quit practicing and taking piano lessons!

I remember the fun we had every Halloween with you, Pat, and Julie, driving to all the neighbors and relatives to go Trick or Treating! Ralph and Opal Wheatly would let you kids grab a handful of pennies from their penny jar instead of handing out candy. You thought that was the greatest thing ever. Those days, you kids would get homemade popcorn balls, homemade candy, full size candy bars, and even brown bags with candy. We would drive a lot of miles and visit a lot of relatives, but the drive was always worth the prize!

I remember living in the one room schoolhouse, and you and Pat would spend hours outside playing in the dirt "farming." Dad made you some homemade farming equipment to pull behind your tractors. I loved those years living there.

I remember more than one summer replacing the kitchen window (at the schoolhouse) because it would get broken while you and Pat practiced playing baseball in the yard.

I also remember the fun it was preparing for and participating in your Jr. and Sr. Proms! Raising funds for the after-prom parties, ordering tuxes, buying flowers, washing cars, renting cars, decorating … and the pictures, oh my all the pictures! You and Jen looked amazing!

# AFTERWORD

I've had an amazing life! I can't think of anything I regret or anything I would change. Yes, I now have this illness, but I'm facing it with the same gusto, the same positive attitude I've had my entire life.

To all who have read this book, I encourage you—no, I'm telling you!—to stay positive, no matter what comes your way. When the dark times come, rest assured they will come to an end at some point. And when you're in the good times … enjoy them to the fullest—that's the only way to live life!

I love you all!,
**Tim Schut**